Bottlenose Dolphin Training and Interaction

SeaWorld
ADVENTURE PARKS

Busch
GARDENS

DISCOVERY COVE.

Dolphin Discovery

Bottlenose Dolphin Training and Interaction

PART OF THE SEAWORLD EDUCATION SERIES

Research/Writing/Layout
Deborah Nuzzolo

Technical Advisors
Brad Andrews
Dave Force
John Kerivan
Thad Lacinak
Daniel K. Odell, Ph.D.
Julie Scardina
Mike Scarpuzzi
Chuck Tompkins
Dudley Wigdahl
Glenn Young

Education Directors
Hollis J. Gillespie
John Lowe
Scott Rogers
Sheila Voss
Joy L. Wolf

Editorial Staff
Judith Coats
Deborah Nuzzolo
Danielle Oki
Donna Parham
Jody Rake
Tressa Whalen
Loran Wlodarski

Illustrations
Joe Ferrara
Doug Fulton
August Stein

Photos
Mike Aguilera
Bob Couey
Chris Gotshall

Photographs

Cover: This book explores the bottlenose dolphin *Tursiops truncatus*.

Title page: Bottlenose dolphins leap and dive in the SeaWorld Rocky Point Preserve habitat.

Page 1: The bottlenose dolphin is probably the most well known dolphin species.

Pages 30–31: SeaWorld's animal training program is based on a foundation of strong, positive relationships with the animals and an environment they "enjoy."

Pages 58–59: A Discovery Cove guest enters the watery world of the bottlenose dolphin. SeaWorld and Discovery Cove dolphin interaction programs offer safe, positive experiences for both human and dolphin participants.

©2003 Sea World, Inc. All Rights Reserved.

Published by the SeaWorld Education Department
500 Sea World Drive, San Diego, California, 92109-7904

No part of this publication may be reproduced or transmitted in any form or by any means without permission in writing from the publisher.

ISBN 1-893698-03-3
Printed in the United States of America.

Contents

The Bottlenose Dolphin

"Diviner than the dolphin is nothing yet created..."

Oppian

Dolphins and people have a long history of interaction.

Mythical Connections

The human-dolphin connection has existed for centuries. Myths and art of the ancient Greeks provide us with numerous instances of dolphins as rescuers, messengers, and companions. In fact, it was believed that dolphins befriended humans because dolphins were once human themselves.

For the early Greek sailors, the sea inspired fear; some believed the sea led to the edge of the earth. As myths were created to interpret the natural world and explain the unknown, the sea became a source of divine power. Myths featured gods with human traits and supernatural abilities. Dolphins often played important roles in human and god interplay. Here are some dolphin myths:

Dolphin origin. According to a Greek myth, the child god Dionysus hires a ship to sail from Icaria to Naxos, his home. But once on board, Dionysus discovers that the crew intends to sail to Egypt and sell him as a slave. Dionysus uses his divine powers to transform the ship—vines wrap the ship's sails, mast, and sides. The sailors, terrified, jump into the ocean and become dolphins.

Dolphin rescuer. While sailing home to Corinth, the famous poet/musician Arion discovers that the ship's crew intends to rob him of his wealth and life. Arion sings one last song and jumps overboard. A dolphin, attracted by the song, rescues Arion and carries him safely to shore.

Dolphin companion. A dolphin, injured by fishermen, is saved by a boy. In gratitude, the dolphin befriends the boy and carries him whenever he wants a ride.

Dolphins in human-god interplay. Poseidon, Greek god of the sea, commands the ocean and everything in it. Poseidon's sacred symbol of a serene sea is the dolphin. When Poseidon falls in love with Amphitrite he sends one of his dolphins to find her and persuade her to marry Poseidon.

Apollo, in the form of a dolphin, leaps onto a Cretan ship and brings the sailors to Delphi, where he appoints them priests of his temple. (The Greek word for dolphin is *delphis*.)

From sea to sky.

Most star constellations link to ancient Greek or Roman myths. One such constellation is Delphinus, "The Dolphin." The inspiration for its name is attributed to various Greek myths including two mentioned above: the dolphin who united Poseidon and Amphitrite or the dolphin that saved Arion.

The ancient Greeks explained their world through their myths. Ancient Greece was a seafaring nation, so it's not surprising that dolphins were significant in their poetry, art, and religion. Even today with all of our scientific knowledge, dolphins inspire intrigue.

Ancient Greek myths provide us with numerous instances of dolphins as rescuers, messengers, and companions.

Dolphins In-depth

Through observation and scientific study we know that dolphins did not originate from people as told in Greek mythology. However, we are connected. Dolphins are warm-blooded, air-breathing mammals just like people—but in a group all their own. Dolphins, porpoises, and whales belong to the scientific order Cetacea. Cetacea is derived from the Greek word for "a whale." Cetaceans are further divided into three suborders: Odontoceti (toothed whales), Mysticeti (baleen whales), and Archaeoceti (extinct whales of which only fossils remain). Scientists group most dolphins (about 30 species) in the scientific family Delphinidae, part of the suborder Odontoceti.

Despite the bottlenose dolphin's worldwide distribution, most scientists currently recognize only one species. But recent advances in molecular biology are providing new information.

Delphinids include such well known dolphins as bottlenose dolphins and common dolphins as well as pilot whales, killer whales, and false killer whales. This book will discuss the bottlenose dolphin, *Tursiops truncatus*.

Distribution and habitat.

The bottlenose dolphin lives in temperate and tropical waters worldwide. Coastal bottlenose dolphins live close to land and frequent harbors, bays, lagoons, gulfs, and estuaries. Oceanic dolphins live farther out at sea. Many dolphins have a home range, an area where they tend to stay. Others migrate; variations in water temperature, movements of food fish, and feeding habits may account for seasonal movements of some dolphins to and from certain areas.

5

Population.

The worldwide population of bottlenose dolphins is unknown. Specific bottlenose dolphin populations in a few areas have been estimated. U.S. National Marine Fisheries Service (NMFS) surveys estimate 243,500 bottlenose dolphins in the eastern tropical Pacific. NMFS surveys in the northern Gulf of Mexico estimate 35,000 to 45,000 bottlenose dolphins. In U.S. waters of the western North Atlantic, aerial surveys estimate 10,000 to 13,000 individuals. Bottlenose dolphins are not endangered.

Size.

Despite this dolphin's worldwide distribution, most scientists currently recognize only one species. Bottlenose dolphins measured off Sarasota, Florida average 2.5 to 2.7 m (8.2–8.9 ft.) and weigh between 190 and 260 kg (419–573 lb.). Large bottlenose dolphins in the Pacific Ocean may be 3.7 m (12 ft.) and weigh 454 kg (1,000 lb.). On average, full grown males are slightly longer than females, and considerably heavier.

Physical features.

The dolphin's sleek, fusiform body, together with its flippers, flukes, and dorsal fin, adapt this mammal for ocean life. A dolphin's forelimbs are pectoral flippers. Pectoral flippers have the major skeletal elements of land mammal forelimbs, but are foreshortened and modified. As it swims, a dolphin uses its pectoral flippers to steer and, with the help of the flukes, to stop.

A bottlenose dolphin has a broad skull and short rostrum. Teeth are conical and interlocking.

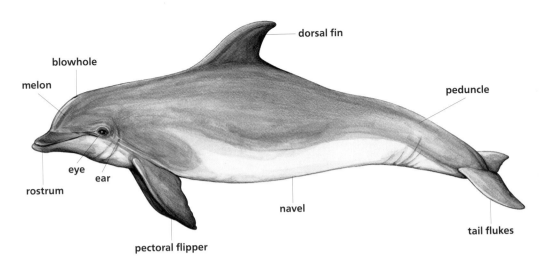

The bottlenose dolphin, like other whales, has forelimbs modified into flippers, a horizontally flattened tail, a nostril at the top of the head for breathing, and no hind limbs. The dolphin's streamlined shape glides easily through water and helps the dolphin conserve energy as it swims.

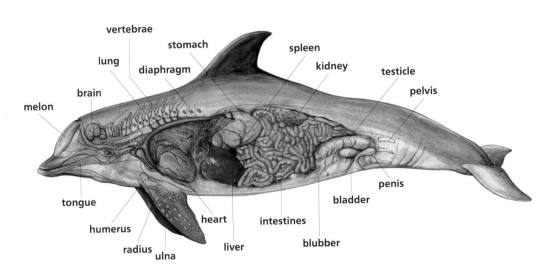

Take a look inside a male bottlenose dolphin. Dolphins and other whales are warm-blooded, with a core body temperature about the same as ours. Because they live in cool water, they have adaptations for retaining body heat. A thick layer of fatty tissue–called blubber–lies just under the skin. Blubber insulates a dolphin's internal organs and muscles.

Head Features

A bottlenose dolphin has a well defined rostrum (snoutlike projection), usually about 7–8 cm (3 in.) long, marked by a lateral crease. The dolphin's teeth are conical and interlocking, designed for grasping, not chewing, food. The number of teeth varies considerably among dolphin individuals. Most individuals have 20 to 25 teeth on each side of the upper jaw and 18 to 24 teeth on each side of the lower jaw, a total of 76 to 98 teeth.

A dolphin's eyes are on the sides of the head, near the corners of the mouth. Glands at the inner corners of the eye sockets secrete an oily, jellylike mucus that lubricates the eyes, washes away debris, and probably helps streamline a dolphin's eye as it swims. This tearlike film may also protect the eyes from infective organisms. Dolphins have acute vision both in and out of the water. A dolphin's eye is particularly adapted for seeing under water.

Ears, located just behind the eyes, are small inconspicuous openings, with no external flaps. Dolphins have a well developed, acute sense of hearing. Bottlenose dolphins hear tones within the frequency range of 1 to 150 kHz. For comparison, the average human hearing range is about 0.02 to 17 kHz. A bottlenose dolphin hears best in the 40 to 100 kHz range. Dolphins can detect sound frequencies below 1 kHz if loud enough.

A bottlenose dolphin routinely swims at speeds of about 5 to 11 kph (3–7 mph).

Each lobe of a dolphin's tail is called a fluke. Flukes are flattened pads of tough, dense, fibrous connective tissue, completely without bone, cartilage, or muscle. A dolphin uses the powerful muscles along its back and tail stalk to move the flukes up and down. This motion moves the dolphin forward through the water.

Like the flukes, the dorsal fin has no bone, cartilage, or muscle inside. The dorsal fin may act as a keel. It probably helps stabilize a dolphin as it swims, but is not essential to a dolphin's balance.

A bottlenose dolphin's color is gray to dark gray on its back, fading to white on its belly. This coloration, a type of camouflage known as countershading, may help conceal a dolphin from predators and prey.

Swimming.

Bottlenose dolphins routinely swim at speeds of about 5 to 11 kph (3–7 mph). Ergometric (exercise) studies indicate burst (maximum) speeds of 29 to 35 kph (18–22 mph). Swimming speed and duration are closely tied: high-speed swimming probably lasts only seconds while low-speed swimming may last for long periods of time.

Dolphin Diving

Depending on habitat, most bottlenose dolphins regularly dive to depths of 3 to 46 m (10–150 ft.). They are, however, capable of diving to greater depths. Under experimental conditions, the deepest trained dive is 547 m (1,795 ft.). On average, a dive may last eight to ten minutes.

Countershading allows a dolphin's back to blend into the dark ocean depths, and its underside to blend with the lighter ocean surface.

All marine mammals have special physiological adaptations for diving. These adaptations enable a dolphin to conserve oxygen. For example, dolphins, like other marine mammals, have a slower heart rate while diving. When diving, blood is shunted away from tissues tolerant of low oxygen levels toward the heart, lungs, and brain, where oxygen is needed. Additionally, the muscle of bottlenose dolphins has a high content of the oxygen-binding protein myoglobin. Myoglobin stores oxygen and helps prevent muscle oxygen deficiency.

A bottlenose dolphin breathes through a single blowhole located on the dorsal surface of its head. The blowhole is covered by a muscular flap, which provides a watertight seal. When the blowhole is closed, the muscle is relaxed. To open the blowhole, a dolphin contracts the muscle. A dolphin holds its breath while below water. It opens its blowhole and begins to exhale just before reaching the surface of the water. At the surface, the dolphin quickly inhales and then relaxes the muscular flap to close it.

muscular flap

Below water, the muscular flap covering the blowhole provides a watertight seal.

The visible blow of a dolphin is formed by both seawater that has collected around the blowhole and the water vapor condensing in the respiratory gases as they expand in the cooler air.

As a dolphin exhales, seawater that has collected around the blowhole is carried up with the respiratory gases. Seawater and the water vapor condensing in the respiratory gases as they expand in the cooler air form the visible blow of a dolphin. During each respiration a dolphin exchanges 80% or more of its lung air. (This is much more efficient than in humans, who exchange only about 17% of their lung air with each breath.) Exhaling and inhaling take about 0.3 seconds. A bottlenose dolphin's average respiratory rate is about two to three breaths per minute.

The bottlenose dolphin's streamlined body, together with its flippers, flukes, and dorsal fin, adapt this mammal for life in an aquatic environment.

Thermoregulation

A dolphin's core body temperature is about 36.9°C (98.4°F). Dolphins have several thermoregulatory strategies to help them maintain their core temperature, including body shape, blubber, and countercurrent heat exchange.

Body shape. Their fusiform body shape and reduced limb size decrease the amount of surface area exposed to the external environment. This helps dolphins conserve body heat. Dolphins adapted to cooler, deeper water generally have larger bodies and smaller flippers than do coastal dolphins, further reducing the ratio of surface area to overall body mass.

Blubber. Lying just underneath a dolphin's skin is a thick blubber layer. Dolphins deposit most of their body fat here. Blubber insulates the dolphin and streamlines the body.

It also functions as an energy reserve. A bottlenose dolphin's body fat generally accounts for about 18% to 20% of its body weight.

Countercurrent heat exchange. A bottlenose dolphin's circulatory system adjusts to conserve or dissipate body heat and maintain body temperature. Arteries in the flippers, flukes, and dorsal fin are surrounded by veins. Thus, some heat from the blood traveling through the arteries is transferred to the venous blood rather than the environment. This countercurrent heat exchange aids dolphins in conserving body heat.

Additionally, when a dolphin dives, blood is shunted away from the surface of the body. This decrease in circulation also conserves body heat.

During prolonged exercise or in warm water a dolphin may need to shed excess heat. In this case, circulation increases to blood vessels near the surface of the flippers, flukes, and dorsal fin, and decreases to blood vessels circulating blood to the body core.

Other strategies. In general, bottlenose dolphins have a higher metabolic rate than land mammals of similar size. This increased metabolism generates a great deal of body heat. Mammals lose body heat when they exhale. But dolphins conserve a considerable amount of heat because they breathe less frequently than land mammals.

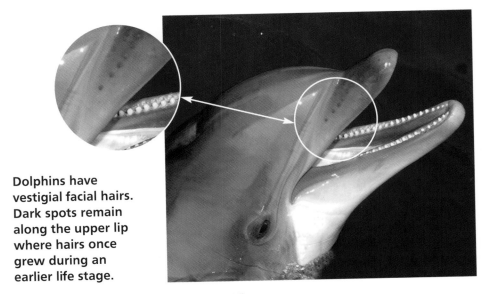

Dolphins have vestigial facial hairs. Dark spots remain along the upper lip where hairs once grew during an earlier life stage.

Dolphin Calves

Dolphin calves are born in the water, usually tail-first; but head-first deliveries are also seen. At birth, calves are about 106 to 132 cm (42–52 in.) long and weigh about 20 kg (44 lb.). In the first few days after birth, the calf's dorsal fin and tail flukes are pliable and lack firmness, but gradually stiffen. Calves, darker than adults, show several vertical, light lines on their sides, a result of fetal folding. These lines disappear within six months.

Nursing usually begins within six hours of birth. Calves nurse under water, close to the surface. The calf suckles from nipples concealed in abdominal mammary slits. Milk is composed of 33% fat, 6.8% protein, and 58% water, with traces of lactose. The rich milk helps the baby rapidly develop a thick blubber layer. A calf may nurse for up to 18 months. In caring for her calf, a mother dolphin stays close by and attentively directs the

calf's movements. The calf is carried in the mother's "slip stream," the hydro-dynamic wake that develops as the mother swims. This helps the baby swim and enables the mother and calf to stay up with the group. Worldwide, bottlenose dolphin calves are born throughout the year. Gestation is about 12 months. A female dolphin can potentially bear a calf every two years, but calving intervals generally average three years.

Bottlenose dolphins are active to some degree both day and night; activities include feeding, socializing, traveling, and resting. How often activities occur and how long they last vary with time of day, season, habitat, and other factors.

Social structure.

Bottlenose dolphins live in fluid social groups. Although some dolphins may repeatedly associate with one another, these associations are rarely permanent. In the past, bottlenose dolphin groups have been referred to as pods—social groups of unchanging composition. For example, killer whales live in long-term social groups; killer whale pods usually consist of males, females, and calves of varying ages. Long-term studies of bottlenose dolphins have now shown that their group composition is changeable.

In the wild, group composition and structure are based largely on age, sex, and reproductive condition. Bottlenose dolphins show patterns of association—basic group types include nursery groups (mothers and their most recent offspring), juveniles, and adult males.

A calf typically stays with its mother three to six years or more.

Dolphin calves are born in the water, usually tail-first.

In general, group size tends to increase with water depth and openness of habitat. This may correlate with foraging strategies and protection. Bottlenose dolphins commonly swim in groups of 2 to 15 individuals. Several groups may temporarily join (for several minutes or hours) in open ocean waters to form larger groups during which the dolphins may change associates.

Social behavior.

Some group members establish strong social bonds. Mother-calf bonds are long-lasting; a calf typically stays with its mother three to six years or more. Adult male pair bonds are strong and long-lasting. Male pairs often engage in a number of cooperative behaviors. Bonds between males and females are short-lived, and female-female bonds are not very strong.

Social behavior comprises a major portion of the dolphins' daily activities. They establish and maintain dominance by biting, chasing, jaw-clapping, and smacking their tails on the water. Dolphins often show aggression by scratching one another with their teeth, leaving superficial lacerations that soon heal. Traces of light parallel stripes remain on the skin. These marks are seen in virtually all dolphin species. They also show aggression by emitting bubble clouds from blowholes. During courtship, dolphins engage in head-butting and tooth-scratching.

A breach is a behavior in which a dolphin jumps out of the water and lands on its side, belly, or back.

Individual behavior.

Riding the bow waves or stern wakes of boats is probably adapted from the natural behavior of riding ocean swells, the wakes of large whales, or a mother dolphin's "slip stream" (hydrodynamic wake). Dolphins have been seen jumping as high as 4.9 m (16 ft.) from the water surface and landing on their backs, bellies, or sides in a behavior called a breach. Both young and old dolphins chase one another, carry objects around, toss seaweed to each other, and use objects to solicit interaction. Such activity may be practice for catching food.

Food and Feeding

Dolphins are active predators and eat a wide variety of fishes, squids, and crustaceans such as shrimps. The foods available to a dolphin vary with its geographic location. Dolphins do not chew their food. Usually they swallow fish whole, head first, so the fish spines won't catch in their throats. They break larger fish by shaking them or rubbing them on the ocean floor. Adult bottlenose dolphins eat approximately 4% to 5% of their body weight in food per day. A nursing mother's daily intake is considerably higher: about 8%.

Hunting strategies.

Hunting strategies are varied and diverse. Bottlenose dolphins often cooperate when hunting and catching fish. In open waters, a dolphin group sometimes encircles a large school of fish and herds the fish into a small, dense mass, sometimes using their tail flukes to stun the fish. The dolphins take turns charging through the school to feed. Occasionally dolphins herd fish against a sand bar or shoreline to trap them in shallow water where the fish are easy prey. Dolphins also feed on individual, nonschooling fishes. To hunt larger fishes, a bottlenose dolphin may use its tail flukes to flip a fish out of the water, then retrieve the stunned prey.

Taste and smell.

Little is known about a dolphin's sense of taste. Features of the brain and cranial nerves suggest they may have some sort of a taste sensation. Bottlenose dolphins have taste buds, but they haven't been extensively studied. Olfactory lobes of the brain and olfactory nerves are absent, indicating no sense of smell.

Adult bottlenose dolphins eat about 4% to 5% of their body weight in food per day.

Bottlenose dolphins, identify themselves with a signature whistle.

Sound in the Sea

Dolphins rely heavily on sound production and reception to navigate, communicate, and hunt in dark or murky waters. Under these conditions, sight is of little use.

Bottlenose dolphins identify themselves with a signature whistle. For example, a mother dolphin may whistle to her calf almost continually for several days after giving birth. This acoustic imprinting helps the calf learn to identify its mother. Besides whistles, bottlenose dolphins produce clicks and sounds that resemble moans, trills, grunts, and squeaks. They make these sounds at any time and at considerable depths.

Sounds vary in volume, wavelength, frequency, and pattern. Scientists have found no evidence of a dolphin language.

As with all toothed whales, a dolphin's larynx does not have vocal cords, but researchers have theorized that at least some sound production originates in the larynx. Early studies suggested that "whistles" were generated in the larynx while "clicks" were produced in the nasal sac region. Bottlenose dolphins can produce both clicks and whistles at the same time.

Technological advances in bioacoustic research enable scientists to better explore the nasal region. Studies suggest that a tissue complex in the nasal region is the most likely site of all sound production. Sounds are probably produced by movements of

Acoustic imprinting helps a dolphin calf learn to identify its mother.

air in the trachea and nasal sacs. Bottlenose dolphins produce sounds ranging from 0.25 to 150 kHz. The lower frequency vocalizations (0.25 to 50 kHz) are likely used in social communication. Higher frequency clicks (40 to 150 kHz) are primarily used in echolocation.

Echolocation.

Dolphins possess the ability to echolocate; they can locate and discriminate objects by projecting high-frequency sound waves and listening for echoes. Dolphins echolocate by producing clicking sounds and then receiving and interpreting the resulting echo. Bottlenose dolphins produce directional, broadband clicks in trains. Each click lasts about 50 to 128 microseconds. The click trains pass through the melon (rounded region of a dolphin's forehead), which consists of lipids (fats). The melon acts as an acoustical lens to focus these sound waves into a beam, which is projected forward into water in front of the animal.

Sound waves travel through water at a speed of about 1.5 km/sec (0.9 mi./sec.), which is 4.5 times faster than sound traveling through air. These sound waves bounce off objects in the water and return to the dolphin in the form of an echo. The major areas of sound reception are the fat-filled cavities of the lower jaw bones. Sounds are received and conducted through the lower jaw to the middle ear, inner ear, and then to hearing centers in the brain via the auditory nerve. The brain receives the sound waves in the form of nerve impulses, which relay the messages of sound and enable the dolphin to interpret the sound's meaning.

By this complex system of echolocation, dolphins can determine size, shape, speed, distance, direction, and even some of the internal structure of objects in the water. They are able to learn and later recognize the echo signatures returned by preferred prey species.

Despite the effectiveness of echolocation, studies show that a visually deprived dolphin takes more time to echolocate on an object than a dolphin using vision in tandem with echolocation. Many of the details of echolocation are not completely understood. Research on echolocation continues.

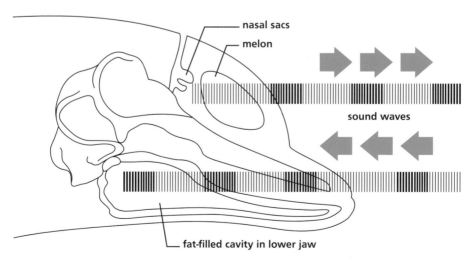

Bottlenose dolphins echolocate by producing high-frequency clicks that pass through the melon, then receiving and interpreting the resulting echo.

A bottlenose dolphin's average life span is probably 20 years or less. This estimate is based on census data from the bottlenose dolphin population off the coast of Sarasota, Florida. The Sarasota Dolphin Research Project (SDRP) is the longest-running study of wild dolphins in the world.

SDRP studies have shown that dolphins can live into their 40s; a few females have even lived past 50. This appears to be a maximum age, comparable to a human living to be about 100. Only 1% to 2% of dolphins reach that age.

As a dolphin ages, it periodically produces growth layer groups of dental material. Age can be estimated by examining a sliced section of a tooth and counting these layers. Scientists have developed several tooth analysis methods. Some of these methods can be accurate and reliable.

Causes of death.

Natural predators include certain large shark species such as tiger sharks, dusky sharks, bull sharks, and great white sharks. Killer whales may occasionally prey on bottlenose dolphins, but documented cases are rare.

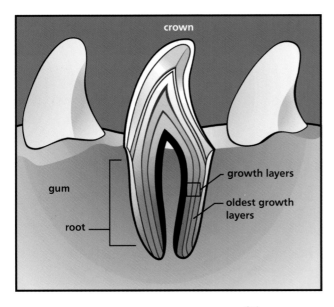

Age can be estimated by examining a sliced section of a tooth and counting growth layer groups of dental material.

A bottlenose dolphin's average life span is probably 20 years or less. Studies have shown that dolphins can live into their 40s. This appears to be a maximum age, comparable to a human living to be about 100.

As in any animal population, a variety of diseases and parasites also can be responsible for dolphin deaths. Dolphins may suffer from viral, bacterial, and fungal infections. In addition, they may develop stomach ulcers, skin diseases, tumors, heart disease, urogenital disorders, and respiratory disorders. Parasites that typically affect dolphins include tapeworms, flukes, and roundworms.

Strandings.

In 1987 and 1998, more than 740 dead bottlenose dolphins washed ashore on the east coast of the United States. Scientists originally believed that the dolphin deaths were triggered by a naturally occurring "red tide" toxin (originating in small marine organisms called dinoflagellates) combined with bacterial and viral infections. Further analysis concluded that morbillivirus caused the deaths.

27

Human impact.

In the past, bottlenose dolphins have been taken directly for meat, leather, oil, and meal (for fertilizer and animal feed). Directed takes still occur in various parts of the world including Peru, Sri Lanka, and Japan. Dolphins also are caught accidentally in fishing gear during commercial fishing operations.

Yet even where they're not hunted, dolphins are threatened by some human activities. Dolphins, particularly coastal animals, are affected by heavy boat traffic, habitat destruction, competition with fisheries, and pollution. Industrial and agricultural pollutants in coastal habitats have resulted in high levels of toxins in the water and high concentrations of toxins in dolphin tissues.

Legal Protection

Convention on International Trade in Endangered Species of Wild Fauna and Flora (CITES). CITES convened in 1973 in Washington D.C. and became effective in 1975. This international treaty regulates trade in certain wildlife species. All toothed whales, including bottlenose dolphins, are listed on CITES Appendix II. Appendix II includes species identified as threatened, or likely to become endangered if trade isn't regulated.

IUCN/The World Conservation Union. The IUCN Species Survival Commission Cetacean Specialist Group Action Plan includes projects related to bottlenose dolphin conservation, such as studies of accidental entanglement.

U.S. Marine Mammal Protection Act (MMPA). Dolphins are protected by the MMPA. This 1972 Act made it illegal to hunt or harass any marine mammal in U.S. waters. The MMPA does allow for certain exceptions: native subsistence hunting; collecting or temporarily restraining marine mammals for research, education, and public display; and taking restricted numbers of marine mammals incidentally in the course of fishing operations. The primary objective of the MMPA is to maintain marine ecosystem health and stability, and to obtain and maintain optimum sustainable marine mammal populations. According to the MMPA, all whales and dolphins in U.S. waters are under the jurisdiction of the National Marine Fisheries Service, a division of the U.S. Department of Commerce. ➤

Dolphins, particularly coastal animals, are affected by heavy boat traffic, habitat destruction, competition with fisheries, and pollution.

Dolphin Training

"The three most important concepts in animal training are: to build positive relationships, to draw lots of attention to desirable behavior and to make it fun for both you and the animals.

...Training animals is a combination of the science of learning theory and the art of applying those principles most effectively in different situations with different animals."

Julie Scardina, SeaWorld/Busch Gardens Animal Ambassador

Successful training at SeaWorld involves building a strong and rewarding relationship between trainer and animal.

Basic Training

SeaWorld's animal training foundation is based on strong, positive relationships with the animals in an environment that they "enjoy" being a part of. Three important steps—reinforcers, communication, and target recognition—are the basic building blocks of how SeaWorld trains dolphins and other animals.

Reinforcers.

When a dolphin performs a particular behavior and the consequences of that behavior are in some way favorable to that dolphin, the dolphin is likely to repeat that behavior. The consequence is reinforcing. Stimuli (changes in the environment that produce a behavioral response) that strengthen behavior are called reinforcers.

For example, if the dolphin splashes a guest, any of several consequences may follow: the guest becomes wet, the guest jumps backward, the crowd cheers. If any of these consequences are reinforcing to the dolphin, it is likely to repeat the splashing behavior. This type of learning, in which the likelihood of behaviors are increased or decreased by the consequences that follow them, is called operant conditioning.

When a dolphin performs a correct behavior, the trainer may deliver a positive reinforcer. As a result, the dolphin is likely to increase the frequency of that particular behavior. For example, if the dolphin leaps into the air and a reinforcer follows, the behavior of leaping is likely to increase in frequency under the same conditions.

Humans learn by the same principles. For example, consider the behavior of students answering questions in a classroom. If the behavior is reinforced by attention and praise, students are likely to repeat the behavior (even if the answer is not correct). If no reinforcement (positive attention) were to follow, repeating that behavior would be less likely.

SeaWorld trainers use positive reinforcement to train dolphins and other animals. All training is based on reinforcing desired behaviors and not reinforcing undesired behaviors. Reinforcers motivate a dolphin to repeat desired behaviors. A variety of interesting, stimulating reinforcers is the key to training dolphins at SeaWorld.

A reinforcer can be anything the dolphin may perceive as favorable, including touch. A bottlenose dolphin's skin appears to be sensitive to a broad range of tactile sensations.

33

Reinforcers can be anything that the dolphin may perceive as favorable. A back scratch, a toy, a fish, or a favorite activity all are examples of positive reinforcers. Other reinforcing stimuli for SeaWorld animals include being touched; being squirted with a water hose; being rubbed down; playing with ice or floats; and other visual, auditory, and tactile stimulation.

Each dolphin may not respond in the same way to the same reinforcer. Therefore, trainers must learn which reinforcers are appropriate for individual animals. Trainers determine what is reinforcing to the animals by carefully observing the frequency of behavior after a particular reinforcer is applied. If

Reinforcers let the animals know when they have performed the desired behavior. For example, if a dolphin leaps into the air and a reinforcer follows, the behavior of leaping is likely to increase in frequency under the same conditions.

the frequency decreases, trainers assume that the consequence was not reinforcing; therefore, they try a different reinforcer. On the other hand, if a dolphin responds by soliciting or appearing to desire a particular stimulus, that stimulus is likely to be an effective positive reinforcer.

Some reinforcers may be intrinsically rewarding, such as food. SeaWorld trainers use food, a primary reinforcer, more frequently during the early stages of the training process. Not all reinforcers are automatically rewarding. Some must be trained to be effective. Often new reinforcers can be trained by pairing the unfamiliar stimulus, such as a toy, with a known positive reinforcer. Eventually, through repeated pairing, the unfamiliar stimulus (toy) becomes positive to the dolphin, and therefore an effective new reinforcer. It has become a conditioned reinforcer. Trainers continually learn about the relationships between reinforcers and behaviors through direct contact and observation of the dolphins. Daily data recording contributes to the pool of knowledge regarding dolphin behavior as well as their ability to learn.

SeaWorld animals are trained on a variable ratio reinforcement schedule. Variable ratio reinforcement occurs after a certain number of responses: animals are not automatically reinforced after each behavior. The number of responses, however, varies unpredictably from occasion to occasion. Variable ratio schedules produce higher response rates than other reinforcement schedules.

Communication.

Reinforcers are one way to communicate with dolphins. Reinforcers let the dolphin know when it has performed the desired behavior. A delay of even a few seconds may accidentally reinforce an undesired behavior. Because it is not always possible to instantly reinforce a dolphin while it is performing, a signal is useful to tell the dolphin that it has performed correctly, and that it may receive further reinforcement.

Food, a primary reinforcer, is used more frequently during the early stages of the training process.

Each dolphin is trained to recognize a bridge signal. A bridge signal lets the dolphin know it has performed correctly. A whistle is a common bridge signal used in dolphin training.

The signal reinforces the instant the dolphin performs the correct behavior and is the stimulus for the dolphin to return to the trainer. This signal is called a bridge signal. The dolphin learns that when it hears, feels, or sees a bridge signal it has performed the behavior correctly and needs to return to the trainer to receive further reinforcement or another signal.

Each dolphin is trained to recognize a bridge signal. Before a dolphin receives a reinforcer, a bridge signal is introduced (usually a whistle or a light touch). The dolphin comes to associate the bridge signal with being reinforced. The bridge signal becomes a conditioned reinforcer. It remains reinforcing through random association with primary and other secondary reinforcers.

A Training Career

A career as a SeaWorld animal trainer offers the unique and exciting opportunity to work directly with dolphins and other marine mammals. However, a limited number of job openings are available, and if you are considering training as a career goal you should prepare by pursuing the appropriate education and experience. Applicants are expected to have academic coursework in zoology, marine biology, and animal behavior or psychology. Prior animal training experience or experience working with animals is preferred. Public speaking or performance experience is also desirable. Since SeaWorld trainers work in and around water, strong swimming skills are essential. Applicants must pass a rigorous swim test, which includes a 67-m (220-ft.) freestyle swim and a 7.3-m (24-ft.) free dive to retrieve a small weight. SeaWorld trainers are certified in scuba diving, CPR and first aid. Due to the specialized nature of the work, a year-long, on-the-job apprenticeship training period familiarizes trainers with SeaWorld animal care and training methods. A trainer must have a great deal of patience and excellent communication skills. But perhaps the most important quality for success in animal training is the ability to work effectively with people as well as animals.

A SeaWorld trainer gives the hand signal for a high jump. The dolphin is trained to associate this visual stimulus with a behavior it has learned.

More about signals.

In a show, a trainer may request many different behaviors of a dolphin. The dolphin is trained to differentiate, or discriminate, among the situations. Discrimination is the tendency for learned behavior to occur in one situation, but not in others. The trainer provides a stimulus that signals to the dolphin that a reinforcement opportunity will follow the resulting correct behavior. The dolphin is trained to associate a visual, auditory, or tactile stimulus with behaviors it has learned. The dolphin learns to discriminate among signals to determine which behavior the trainer expects.

In the shows, many signals are incorporated into trainers' dialogue and stage gestures. Signals may be so subtle that audiences may believe a dolphin is initiating behavior on its own. Sometimes a dolphin may perform several behaviors in a specific sequence before receiving reinforcement. This connected sequence of behaviors is called a chain. SeaWorld trainers train each behavior segment separately and then link behaviors together. The completion of each behavior becomes the stimulus for the next behavior. The chain is complete when the trainer is able to give an initial signal and the entire chain is performed.

The dolphin is successful in discriminating between signals to determine which behavior the trainer expected.

41

4.

To train a dolphin it is often helpful to lead the dolphin through a behavior in small steps. In these photos (numbers 1 to 3 left and 4 above), a SeaWorld trainer uses a tool called a target to lead the dolphin through a series of steps toward the final goal of turning.

Target recognition.

To train a dolphin it is often helpful to lead the dolphin through a behavior in small steps. SeaWorld trainers use a tool called a target to direct a dolphin toward a position or direction. For most animals, the target used is the trainer's hand or a long pole with a foam float or ball on one end. Other targets include a tap on the glass at the side of the pool or an ice cube tossed into the water.

Each dolphin is trained to follow the target. A trainer touches the target gently to the dolphin. The bridge signal is sounded, and the dolphin is reinforced. This is repeated several times. The next step is to position the target a few inches away from the dolphin. By this time, the dolphin has learned that whenever it touches the target, it gets reinforced, so it moves toward the target and touches it. The bridge signal is immediately sounded, and the dolphin is reinforced. After several successful repetitions, the target is moved still farther away. The process is repeated.

Eventually the dolphin will follow the target. The target may now be used to lead the dolphin through a series of steps to perform complex behaviors.

Shaping.

Most behaviors cannot be learned all at once but develop in steps. This step-by-step learning process is called shaping. Many human behaviors are learned through shaping. For example, when children learn to ride a bicycle, most begin by riding a tricycle. The child graduates to a two-wheeler with training wheels, and eventually masters a larger bicycle, perhaps one with multiple speeds. Each step toward the final goal of riding a bicycle is reinforcing.

A target directs a dolphin toward a position or direction. For most animals, the target used is the trainer's hand or a long pole with a foam float or ball on one end.

Dolphins perform the high jump without a target to direct them. The dolphins were trained in a step-by-step learning process called shaping.

The dolphins learn complex behavior through shaping. Each step in the learning process is called an approximation. A dolphin may be reinforced with a variety of rewards for each successive approximation toward the final goal of the desired trained behavior.

Here is an example of how a dolphin might be trained to do a high jump. First, the dolphin is reinforced for touching a arget on the surface of the water. The trainer raises the target a few inches above the water, and reinforces the animal for touching it. As the dolphin succeeds, the trainer continues to raise the target higher and higher above the water. Eventually the dolphin brings its entire body out of the water. The trainer may reinforce the dolphin at any point during the approximation to encourage the desired response. The trainer continues to raise the target until it is at the high jump level. The dolphin is reinforced along each step toward the final goal of a high jump.

45

Reinforcing a dolphin for calm, attentive behavior following the LRS helps the dolphin learn from its mistakes.

Least Reinforcing Scenario

What happens if a trainer requests a particular behavior and the dolphin does not respond, or the dolphin responds with undesired behavior? At SeaWorld, incorrect behavior is followed by a training technique called the Least Reinforcing Scenario (LRS).

The LRS has two components. The first part is a consequence for incorrect behavior. This occurs when the trainer does not bridge, reinforce, or reward the dolphin for the incorrect behavior. The second part is a stimulus providing opportunity for reward. This involves 2 to 3 seconds during which the trainer is relaxed and attempts no change in the environment. (Changes in the environment may accidentally reinforce the behavior.) This time is a stimulus to the dolphin to remain calm and attentive. This stimulus provides a new opportunity for reward or gives the dolphin an opportunity to perform another behavior that will result in reinforcement.

The LRS helps reduce frustration that might result from the lack of reinforcement and teaches the dolphin to react in some non-aggressive way.

The LRS is not a fixed posture, but instead a flexible system enabling the trainer to deliver the LRS in a variety of contexts. The trainer does not ignore the dolphin but must monitor the dolphin's behavior while doing everything possible not to respond to inappropriate behavior. Reinforcing the dolphin for calm, attentive behavior following the LRS helps the dolphin learn from its mistakes. A dolphin never is forced to respond to a situation, nor is it ever punished. When used consistently, the LRS technique eventually decreases undesired behavior and increases calm and attentive behavior.

Behavior Repertoire

Animals have the potential to learn extensive repertoires of behaviors. An experienced animal may learn as many as 200 behaviors. The process of animal training continues throughout an animal's life. Trainers and animals develop new behaviors and modify current behaviors to keep the animals physically and mentally challenged.

The process of training continues throughout a dolphin's life. Trainers and dolphins develop new behaviors and modify current behaviors to keep the dolphins physically and mentally challenged.

Educational value

Over the years, millions of people have visited marinelife parks such as SeaWorld to watch dolphins and other marine animals in shows. Visitors are not only entertained, but also educated. Marinelife parks teach guests about marine animals, their ecosystems, and conservation measures. Not everyone has the chance to see these animals in the wild. The unique opportunity to observe and learn directly from live animals increases public awareness and appreciation of wildlife. Visitor polls provide clear evidence that marinelife parks, aquariums, and zoos provide guests with a heightened appreciation of the importance of conserving marine mammals and preserving habitats. Polls also indicate that visitors are coming away from their marine mammal experiences with greater overall environmental concern, and also interest in taking environmental action.

The greatest number of park visitors polled selected either interacting with marine mammals or viewing marine mammals at marinelife parks as the most valuable educational tools for learning about marine mammals. A visitor's experience of seeing live marine mammals has a great deal of impact on their appreciation and interest in learning about the animals. Marinelife parks provide both educational and entertainment value.

Through decades of experience, SeaWorld trainers have learned that a variety of interactive sessions contributes to animal enrichment and well-being. Session types include exercise, learning, play, relationship, and shows.

Exercise. Exercise sessions are essential to a dolphin's health and well-being. Exercise sessions consist of high-energy behaviors of varying lengths. Each session is tailored to each dolphin and is based on that animal's daily activity levels.

Learning. Learning sessions involve a formal training process for the dolphins, in which trainers condition specific behaviors. Learning sessions provide a series of challenges that enrich the dolphins' environment while yielding valuable information on learning processes. These sessions are important to the dolphins' continued learning and mental stimulation, a process that never stops.

Play. Play sessions provide time in the day for trainers and dolphins to interact with "games" and "toys" that the dolphins appear to enjoy and participate in enthusiastically.

A variety of interactive sessions contributes to animal enrichment and well-being.

While shows follow a basic format, the behaviors, show animals, show segments, and variable reinforcement schedule constantly change, thereby making each show different for the animals.

Relationship. Relationship sessions allow time for a trainer and dolphin to develop reciprocal trust, which enhances the degree of learning. A trainer spends one-on-one quiet interactive time with the dolphin. In many instances trainers learn new reinforcers by observing the types of activities in which the dolphins frequently engage. A strong, rewarding relationship between trainer and dolphin is an important part of the animal training foundation.

Shows. Shows are an opportunity for SeaWorld to educate guests about the behavior, physiology, and ecology of marine animals. Education is one of SeaWorld's main goals as a premier zoological institution. Information is shared with guests through entertaining presentations. While the shows follow a basic format, the behaviors, show animals, show segments, and variable reinforcement schedule constantly change, thereby making each show different for the animals. The variability of each show integrates aspects of other types of sessions, providing stimulating and entertaining interactions.

51

Creating changes in a dolphin's daily activities, such as performing with other animals, provides enrichment. Here, bottlenose dolphins perform with false killer whales (*Pseudorca crassidens*).

Environmental Enrichments

Trainers at SeaWorld aim to create an increasingly complex and stimulating environment to help foster the proper care and management of the dolphins, their habitat, and their behavior.

One enrichment technique is to create changes in a dolphin's daily activities, giving them variety. Dolphins are provided with activities they seem to find interesting and stimulating, including play sessions with trainers and other animals.

To further enhance the positive environment for dolphins and other animals, trainers present them with "toys." These environmental enrichment devices can be used during any type of interaction. Under trainer supervision, the animals interact visually or physically with these environmental enrichment devices.

The many enrichment items vary depending upon the animal. Animals may interact visually with mirrors, brightly colored cones, balls, and animal-shape cut-outs. They may physically interact with floating plastic barrels, large plastic toy hoops, towels, and rubber balls.

This dolphin is trained to present its tail flukes and hold still for blood sampling. Trained husbandry behaviors such as this are vital to evaluating animal health.

Training Benefits

A nimal training provides both educational and entertainment value. Training also benefits animal husbandry and research, and provides physical and mental stimulation for the animals.

Animal husbandry. Animal trainers and veterinary staff work closely together. SeaWorld bases its animal husbandry on a comprehensive preventive medicine program. Direct animal observation is the most useful diagnostic tool. Dolphins also are given regular physical exams, including blowhole cultures and blood and urine analysis. From this information veterinarians usually can detect health concerns early.

To assist with gathering vital health information, the dolphins are trained to present various parts of their bodies for examination, measurement, and blood sampling. They also are trained to hold still during exams, and to urinate when signaled to do so. Trainers and veterinarians also are able to perform delicate procedures, such as taking X-rays and obtaining sonogram data. Training helps veterinarians, animal care specialists, and trainers gather information to form a complete picture of the dolphin's health and maintain detailed husbandry records. The information gained through these routine examinations is a valuable resource for the zoological community.

Research. Training benefits research. By training animals to respond to various stimuli in their environment, researchers can gather scientific information not otherwise available. The information gathered at SeaWorld, combined with the results of field observations, will be instrumental in the conservation of wild populations.

Physical and mental stimulation. In the wild, dolphins are predators and, at the same time, may be prey for other animals. Hunting prey or escaping predators is essential for an animal's survival. Locating, pursuing, and capturing prey, as well as avoiding predators, pose physical and mental challenges for an animal.

At SeaWorld, dolphins neither have to hunt for their food, nor do they have to avoid predators. Instead, SeaWorld's complex, interactive animal habitats and training sessions provide the dolphins with physical and mental stimulation. The play, learning, exercise, relationship, and show sessions provide the dolphins with a variety of challenges.

A SeaWorld trainer weighs a dolphin during a routine examination.

Behavior is anything an animal does involving action and/or a response to stimulation. Behaviors usually are adaptations for survival. Some behaviors are reflexes— unlearned, involuntary, simple responses to specific events. Other behaviors are learned through experience. Scientists define learning as a relatively permanent change in behavior as a result of experience. For the most part, learning occurs gradually and in steps.

An animal learns and is able to adapt to a changing environment. It changes its behavior, learns which responses get desirable results, and changes the frequency of its behavior accordingly.

Animal intelligence. The ability of an animal to process information is based upon its brain anatomy as well as the specific experiences the animal has. Rating the intelligence of different animals is misleading and extremely subjective. In fact, a reliable and consistent intelligence test for humans has yet to be developed. It would be improper to attempt to quantify or qualify the intelligence of animals using only human guidelines.

Are dolphins intelligent? Though we can't evaluate dolphin intelligence using human guidelines, we do know they are well adapted for their environment and have the ability to learn.

56

At SeaWorld, dolphins neither have to hunt for their food, nor do they have to avoid predators. Instead, SeaWorld's complex, interactive animal habitats and training sessions provide the dolphins with physical and mental stimulation.

Dolphin Interaction

"We want our guests to have fun, but we also hope they will leave our parks with a renewed respect for nature and the important role we all can play."

Victor G. Abbey, chairman and president of Busch Entertainment Corporation

U.S. federal laws prohibit people from feeding and swimming with dolphins in the wild.

Wild Interactions

United States federal laws do not permit people to feed and swim with dolphins or other marine mammals in the wild. These actions are considered "harassment." When people try to get close to wild dolphins, whales, seals, and sea lions, they unwittingly put the animals and themselves at risk. Feeding and swimming with marine mammals in the wild is potentially harmful to animals and sometimes dangerous to people.

Because most people will not engage in behavior that they know will hurt animals, the U.S. National Marine Fisheries Service (NMFS), the Alliance of Marine Mammal Parks and Aquariums, and SeaWorld are educating people of the harm caused by disturbing marine mammals or their habitats in the wild. NMFS programs support the domestic and international conservation and management of living marine resources. The Alliance of Marine Mammal Parks and Aquariums is an international association of more than 36 marinelife parks, aquariums, zoos, scientific research facilities, and professional organizations that are dedicated to the conservation of marine mammals and their environments through public display, education, and research.

Altered behavior.

When people feed marine mammals in the wild, the animals may become less able or willing to search for food on their own. A report by the Australian government and American scientists on Western Australia's famous Monkey Mia feeding area shows problems can occur when the public gives food to wild dolphins. Studies found that more than 70% of the infant dolphins born to wild mothers that take fish from people have died. In addition, offspring of dolphins fed at Monkey Mia are less likely to survive long term. Some have suffered from malnutrition. Others are distracted by the feeding and do not pay attention to potential threats from sharks and other predators.

Feeding, swimming with animals, or intruding on wild environments also can have a negative influence on many other normal marine mammal behaviors. People are disturbing dolphin resting areas as well as seal and sea lion rookeries. Scientists believe that the long-term effects of such activities may include the disruption of normal resting patterns, mother-pup nursing and bonding behaviors, and social interactions between animals.

Feeding a dolphin in the wild may make the animal less willing to search for food on its own. Non-natural food items can pose serious health risks.

61

Inappropriate food.

NMFS has serious concerns about the quality of fish being fed to wild marine mammals and has received complaints that animals are being fed harmful items such as sandwiches, cookies, candy, and chips. Fish that has not been inspected for freshness can cause illness in the animals fed. There also is strong evidence that feeding marine mammals in the wild can lead to their learning to steal fish off fishing lines. Animals that have stranded on the beach have been found with hooks and fishing lines in their stomachs.

Injuries.

Reports of injuries to people by marine mammals habituated to being fed in the wild are increasing. Unsuspecting individuals

At marinelife parks, guests learn about dolphins and other marine animals, their ecosystems, and conservation measures. Guests leave with a heightened appreciation of the importance of conserving marine animals and preserving their habitats.

have been bitten, and swimmers have been rammed and pulled under water by wild dolphins that have been taught to expect food from humans.

What can you do?

Share this message with friends, neighbors, and relatives who live by the coast or may be planning trips to ocean resorts. Enjoy professionally managed observation cruises, like whale watching.

Marinelife parks, aquariums, and zoos offer many animal interaction programs that are carefully controlled, monitored by knowledgeable staff, approved by the government, and are safe, positive experiences for both human and animal participants.

Closer Than Ever

Whether feeding a giraffe, sleeping with sharks, or getting splashed by Shamu, guests at SeaWorld, Busch Gardens, and Discovery Cove can get closer than ever to the world's most amazing animals. At Discovery Cove guests play in paradise with dolphins, birds, fishes, and more. SeaWorld provides one-on-one interaction programs with beluga whales, dolphins, and sea lions. At some parks guests can become "trainers for a day," shadowing trainers in their behind-the-scenes work with the animals. Other opportunities include tours of rescue and rehabilitation facilities and joining animal-care experts on rounds. Additionally, thousands of students and teachers visit the parks on instructional field trips and other learning experiences. These visits bring lessons about science, geography, math, and the environment to life. For a more intense and immersive experience, SeaWorld and Busch Gardens Adventure Camps offer hands-on experiences for students. Campers work side-by-side with zoological staff as they help feed everything from penguins to rhinos, learn how to train dolphins or go on rounds with a veterinarian. From shows to camps, in-park attractions to outreach programs, SeaWorld and Busch Gardens are internationally acclaimed for bringing the world of wildlife to millions of people each year.

SeaWorld's Dolphin Interaction Program (DIP), which began in 1995 at SeaWorld San Diego, lets guests enter the watery world of bottlenose dolphins. This program is carefully monitored and supervised by experienced, professional SeaWorld animal trainers. DIP provides safe, positive experiences for both human and animal participants.

The DIP adventure begins with a learning session that introduces participants to the bottlenose dolphin. Guests learn about bottlenose dolphin anatomy, physiology, natural history, husbandry, and training. Then guests gently enter

SeaWorld dolphin interaction programs provide safe, positive experiences for both human and animal participants.

A SeaWorld Dolphin Interaction Program participant gets an incredible eye-to-eye look at a dolphin.

SeaWorld's dolphin interaction pool and wade into the shallow, 60-degree water to meet bottlenose dolphins. Swimming is not required during these shallow-area interactions. DIP participants get an incredible eye-to-eye look at a dolphin, feel the dolphin's smooth skin, give training signals and feed a dolphin.

"Guests love it," says SeaWorld Vice-President of Zoological Operations Mike Scarpuzzi. "They tell us they experienced an incredible connection with the animals — an adventure of a lifetime."

A Discovery Cove guest gets close to a bottlenose dolphin.

Discovery Cove

Discovery Cove in Orlando, Florida opened in July 2000. Here, guests experience exciting animal encounters including swimming and playing with bottlenose dolphins. The dolphin-swim experience begins with an orientation by Discovery Cove's expert trainers and opportunities for participants to ask questions before entering the water. Then everyone wades into shallow water for their introduction to a dolphin.

Participants learn about dolphin behavior, get close to the animals, and find out how Discovery Cove's trainers use hand signals and reinforcement to communicate with the dolphins.

Taking the relationship one step further, guests swim and play with the dolphins one-on-one in a deep-water lagoon. Afterwards, guests can view photographs of their interactions and talk about their dolphin encounter with the trainers and other participants. The entire experience is about 45 minutes long—30 minutes of that time is spent in the water with the bottlenose dolphins.

All of the dolphins at Discovery Cove have been specially selected and trained for guest interaction. The training process is based on positive reinforcement and maintaining a relationship of trust and respect between the animal and its trainers. These same trainers guide guests through their dolphin-swim experiences. Many of the dolphins at Discovery Cove are the product of SeaWorld's breeding program, the most successful such program in the world today.

Guests who participate in the water activities should be comfortable in the water, but need not be exceptional swimmers. Snorkeling lessons are offered throughout the day as well.

SeaWorld, Busch Gardens and Discovery Cove are home to the world's largest zoological collection, totaling some 60,000 animals. These animals serve as ambassadors for their species by helping to entertain, educate and inspire millions of people in and out of the Anheuser-Busch Adventure Parks. ➤

Adventure Camp kids swim, snorkel, and play with a dolphin.

Glossary

behavior — the way an animal acts.

cetacean — any of several large aquatic mammals that have fore-limbs modified into flippers, a horizontally flattened tail, a nostril at the top of the head for breathing, and no hind limbs. Cetaceans include all whales, dolphins, and porpoises.

communicate — to convey information

countershading — a type of camouflage in which the coloration of the dorsal (back) side of an animal is darker than the ventral (belly) side of an animal.

flipper — a broad, flat limb supported by bones and modified for swimming.

flukes — the horizontal lobes of a dolphin's tail, made of connective tissue, not bone.

habitat — the place where an animal lives.

hand signal — a hand movement that communicates to an animal a request to perform a particular behavior.

husbandry — the science and practice of breeding and caring for animals.

learned behavior — behavior that results from experience.

learning — the process by which a change in behavior occurs as a result of experience.

operant conditioning — a type of learning in which behaviors are altered by the consequences that follow them.

reinforce — to strengthen the occurance of a behavior by delivering a positive stimulus or consequence.

reinforcer — a stimulus that strengthens behavior.

response — an activity of an animal that results from a change in the environment.

reward — a reinforcer.

shaping — the step-by-step process of training complex behavior.

stimulus — environmental change that brings about a response from an animal.

target — a focal point that directs an animal toward a position or direction.

thermoregulation — processes by which an animal regulates body temperature.

Bibliography

Bottlenose Dolphins

Au, Whitlow W.L. *The Sonar of Dolphins*. New York: Springer-Verlag, 1993.

Byrum, Jody. *A World Beneath the Waves. Whales, Dolphins, and Porpoises*. San Diego: SeaWorld Education Department Publications, 1998.

Darling, James D., Charles "Flip" Nicklin, Kenneth S. Norris, Hal Whitehead, and Bernd Würsig. *Whales, Dolphins and Porpoises*. Washington D.C.: National Geographic Society, 1995.

Heyning, John. *Whales, Dolphins & Porpoises: Masters of the Ocean Realm*. Seattle: University of Washington Press, 1995.

Leatherwood, Stephen and Randall R. Reeves, eds. *The Bottlenose Dolphin*. San Diego: Academic Press, Inc., 1990.

Minasian, Stanley M., Kenneth C. Balcomb, and Larry Foster. *The World's Whales*. Washington, D.C.: Smithsonian Books, 1984.

Pryor, K. and K.S. Norris, eds. *Dolphin Societies: Discoveries and Puzzles*. Berkeley: University of California Press, 1991.

Reynolds, John E. III, Randall S. Wells, and Samantha D. Eide. *The Bottlenose Dolphin. Biology and Conservation*. Gainesville, Florida: University Press of Florida, 2000.

Ridgway, Sam. *The Dolphin Doctor*. Second edition. New York: Fawcett Crest, 1995.

Thompson, Paul and Ben Wilson. *Bottlenose Dolphins*. Stillwater, Minnesota: Voyageur Press, Inc., 1994.

Wells, Randall S. and Michael D. Scott. "Bottlenose Dolphin *Tursiops truncatus*." In *Handbook of Marine Mammals. Volume 6: The Second Book of Dolphins and the Porpoises*, edited by Sam H. Ridgway and Sir Richard Harrison. San Diego: Academic Press, 1999.

Animal Behavior and Training

Baldwin, John D. and Janice L. Baldwin. *Behavior Principles in Everyday Life*. Second edition. Englewood Cliffs, New Jersey: Prentice Hall, Inc., 1986.

Banks, Edwin M. and John A. Heisey. *Animal Behavior*. Chicago: Educational Methods, 1977.

Chance, Paul. *Learning and Behavior.* Third edition. Pacific Grove, California: Brooks/Cole Publishing Co., 1994.

Ferster, Charles B. and Stuart A. Culbertson. *Behavior Principles.* Englewood Cliffs, New Jersey: Prentice Hall, Inc., 1982.

Goodenough, Judith, Betty McGuire, and Robert Wallace. *Perspectives on Animal Behavior.* New York: John Wiley and Sons, Inc., 1993.

Herman, Louis M., ed. *Cetacean Behavior: Mechanisms and Functions.* New York: John Wiley & Sons, 1980.

International Marine Animal Trainers Association. *Soundings.* Quarterly magazine. Chicago, Illinois.

Kazdin, Alan E. *Behavior Modification in Applied Settings.* Fourth edition. Pacific Grove, California: Brooks/Cole Publishing Company, 1989.

McFarland, David. *Animal Behaviour.* Second edition. Essex, England: Longman Scientific and Technical, 1993.

Nye, Robert D. *What is B.F. Skinner Really Saying?* Englewood Cliffs, New Jersey: Prentice Hall, Inc., 1979.

Pryor, Karen. *Lads Before the Wind. Adventures in Porpoise Training.* New York: Harper & Row, 1975.

Rake, Jody. *Behind the Scenes. Animal Training at SeaWorld, Busch Gardens, and Discovery Cove.* San Diego: SeaWorld, Inc., 2003.

Tinbergen, Niko. *Animal Behavior.* New York: Time-Life Books, 1965.

Web Sites

Animal information from SeaWorld. <www.seaworld.org>

The Alliance of Marine Mammal Parks and Aquariums. <www.ammpa.org>

American Zoo and Aquarium Association. <www.aza.org>

International Marine Animal Trainers Association. <www.imata.org>

NOAA Fisheries/National Marine Fisheries Service. <www.nmfs.noaa.gov>

NOAA Fisheries Office of Protected Resources "Protect Dolphins Campaign." <www.nmfs.noaa.gov/prot_res/MMWatch/protectdolphcamp.html>

Sarasota Dolphin Research Project. <www.brookfieldzoo.org> (Conservation Research section of this Web site.)

The Society for Marine Mammalogy <www.marinemammalogy.org>

Books for Young Readers

Behrens, June. *Dolphins!* Chicago: Children's Press, 1990.

Brust, Beth Wagner. *Zoobooks: Dolphins and Porpoises*. San Diego: Wildlife Education, Ltd., 1999.

George, Twig C. *A Dolphin Named Bob*. New York: HarperCollins Publishers, 1996 (fiction).

Hall, Elizabeth. *Why We Do What We Do. A Look at Psychology*. Boston: Houghton-Mifflin Co., 1973.

Hatherly, Janelle and Delia Nicholls. *Dolphins and Porpoises. Great Creatures of the World*. New York: Facts On File, Inc., 1990.

Kovacs, Deborah. *All About Dolphins!* Bridgeport, Connecticut: Third Story Books, 1994.

Lauber, Patricia. *The Friendly Dolphins*. New York: Scholastic, Inc., 1995.

Nuzzolo, Deborah. *This is a Dolphin*. San Diego: SeaWorld Books for Young Learners/SeaWorld, Inc., 2002.

Orr, Katherine. *Story of a Dolphin*. Minneapolis: Carolrhoda Books, Inc., 1995 (fiction).

Parker, Steve. *Whales and Dolphins*. San Francisco: Sierra Club Books for Children, 1994.

Pringle, Laurence. *Dolphin Man. Exploring the World of Dolphins*. New York: Atheneum Books for Young Readers, 1995.

Reeves, Randall R. and Stephen Leatherwood. *The Sea World Book of Dolphins*. San Diego: Harcourt Brace Jovanovich, Publishers, 1987.

Resnick, Jane. *All About Training Shamu*. Bridgeport, Connecticut: Third Story Books, 1994.

Rinard, Judith E. *Dolphins. Our Friends in the Sea. Dolphins and Other Toothed Whales*. Washington D.C.: The National Geographic Society, 1986.

Stidworthy, John. *Animal Behavior*. New York: Prentice Hall, 1992.

Sweeney, Diane and Michelle Reddy. *Dolphin Babies. Making a Splash*. Niwot, Colorado: Roberts Rinehart Publishers, 1998.

Zinsser, Anne. *Dolphin Magic*. West Cornwall, Connecticut: Locust Hill Press, 1996 (fiction).

Index

The end.

Goals of the SeaWorld and Busch Gardens Education Departments

Based on a long-term commitment to education, SeaWorld and Busch Gardens strive to provide an enthusiastic, imaginative, and intellectually stimulating atmosphere to help students and guests develop a lifelong appreciation, understanding, and stewardship for our environment. Specifically, our goals are...

- To instill in students and guests of all ages an appreciation for science and a respect for all living creatures and habitats.
- To conserve our valuable natural resources by increasing awareness of the interrelationships of humans and the environment.
- To increase students' and guests' basic competencies in science, math, and other disciplines.
- To be an educational resource to the world.

"For in the end we will conserve only what we love. We will love only what we understand. We will understand only what we are taught." — B. Dioum

Want more information?

If you have a question about animals, call 1-800-23-SHAMU (1-800-237-4268). TDD users call 1-800-TD-SHAMU (1-800-837-4268). These toll-free phone numbers are answered by the SeaWorld Education Department.

The SeaWorld Education Department has books, teacher's guides, posters, and videos available on a variety of animals and topics. Call or write to request an Educational Materials catalog or shop online at *swbg-estore.com*

Visit the SeaWorld/Busch Gardens Animal Information Database at *www.seaworld.org* or *www.buschgardens.org*

E-mail: *shamu@seaworld.org*

Anheuser-Busch Adventure Parks

SeaWorld Orlando
(800) 406-2244
7007 Sea World Drive
Orlando, FL 32821-8097

SeaWorld San Antonio
(210) 523-3606
10500 Sea World Drive
San Antonio, TX 78251-3002

SeaWorld San Diego
(800) 380-3202
500 Sea World Drive
San Diego, CA 92109-7904

Discovery Cove
(877) 434-7268
6000 Dicovery Cove Way
Orlando, FL 32821-8097

Busch Gardens Tampa Bay
(813) 987-5555
P.O. Box 9157
Tampa, FL 33674-9157

Busch Gardens Williamsburg
(800) 343-7946
One Busch Gardens Blvd.
Williamsburg, VA 23187-8785